Beginner's Guide to Preparedness

Building Confidence and Security in a Changing World

Millie Copper

Disclaimer

While this book will present a variety of ideas and suggestions, it is for entertainment purposes only and should not be construed as medical advice. Before you begin any physical fitness, mental health, or health changes, you should consult with a professional in that field.

Additionally, the scenarios and strategies discussed are hypothetical and are not guaranteed to work in real-life situations. Individual needs and circumstances can vary greatly, and what may be effective for one person might not be suitable for another. Always prioritize your safety and well-being and seek personalized advice from qualified experts. The information provided in this book is meant to inspire and inform, but it should not replace professional guidance tailored to your specific health and preparedness needs.

Table of Contents

Why Preparedness Matters

Until recently, chances were if the words *prepper* or *preparedness* came up in conversation or in the media, it was to mock or paint a less than flattering picture. Then, just like that, the pandemic happened. Toilet paper, cleansers, canned food, flour, yeast, and a whole variety of other items became scarce. Many people realized maybe those crazy preppers weren't so crazy after all!

The past two years have been a wake-up call for many, and others have been striving to be self-reliant for years.

My husband's grandma, who will be 101 years old later this year, has always kept a full pantry. When I've spoken to her about the Great Depression, she said she didn't really know anything was happening. Her family raised all their own food and were barely affected.

I also have a friend who has been quietly going about their preparedness efforts since the gas shortage of the '70s, and I'm connected in one way or another with dozens of others who have been at this for at least a decade.

Our Preparedness Story

For my family, the Great Coastal Gale of 2007 was our catalyst. High winds took out our power on a Sunday, and we didn't get it back until Saturday. The damage from the wind was extensive. A few days after the lights came back on, there was a mudslide on the highway, closing it for weeks. Things were definitely interesting.

Before the windstorm took out our power, I'm not even sure I'd ever heard the words prepper or preparedness before. I may have heard of survivalists and equated that to the *Rambo* movies.

In those days, I was fairly new to the internet and, while we had a computer, our rural access was still dial-up. For those of you who remember dial-up internet, you may understand why I wasn't on it much! I braved the slow access speeds and started researching "what to do in a power outage" for tips to help us live more comfortably should something similar happen at a future time.

Wow!

Even in late 2007/early 2008, there was a lot of preparedness information. It was very easy to travel down rabbit holes. There was also a lot of mocking. Even as the housing bubble burst and the Great Recession raged, preparedness was an object of ridicule.

Why Prep?

In 2011, National Geographic began airing *Doomsday Preppers*. As each episode focused on different people preparing for "doomsday," they'd ask what they were preparing for. The responses were varied, but most were apocalyptic in nature.

Of course they were! What would be the fun in a show about people who wanted to be able to ride out a windstorm in comfort?

In my opinion, we should all be preppers. None of us know what the future holds. We've seen how quickly things can go from normal to not normal, we've experienced empty store shelves, and we've watched as fuel prices increase. We're experiencing inflation. Our dollars are being stretched to the max. There are conflicts not only in our country but worldwide.

While some preppers may be preparing for an end-of-the-world event, most just want to be able to provide for their family no matter the circumstances.

Over the years, I've met people who lived on their food storage during job loss, the death of a family member, and a spouse's illness. I know people whose car kits have helped at the scene of an accident, whose get-home bag provided comfort when a blizzard closed the interstate. And personally, my version of a bug-out bag was ready to go when we were evacuated for a fast-moving wildfire.

While a localized wind event may not be the fodder for a bestselling novel or movie, the day-to-day mundane is a great reason to prep.

A few reasons you may prep are:

Natural Disasters

- Floods and flash floods: both can cause a disruption of services, property damage, or loss of life
- Heatwaves: can cause power outages and death
- Lightning and summer storms: can cause power outages, wildfires, and more
- Hurricanes, tornadoes, earthquakes, volcanoes, tsunamis: can cause widespread damage in a localized area, power outages, loss of life, disruptions of services, and more
- Winter storms: can cause power outages, travel issues, and loss of water
- Wildfires or forest fires: you may need to evacuate

Personal

A well-stocked pantry is a big help and money saver during personal struggles such as:

- Job loss or a decrease in work
- Health issues, disability, death of a loved one

Localized

- Natural events listed above
- Civil unrest: you may need to hunker down
- Hazardous materials incidents (train wreck, semi-truck overturns): you may need to evacuate or avoid certain areas
- Dam failure, nuclear power plant issues, chemical plants, gas refineries, etc.: you may need to evacuate, or services may be disrupted
- Terrorist acts: certain transportation could be suspended, supply chain issues, etc.

Country-wide or Worldwide

- Pandemic
- Economic issues, inflation
- Wars, the threat of war, issues in other countries that may disrupt our supplies or goods

Everything listed above is realistic and historical. Preparedness doesn't need to be focused on a "the end of the world as we know it" event, commonly called TEOTWAWKI.

About now you may be thinking, "Hey, Millie, don't you write stories about TEOTWAWKI?" While my *Havoc in Wyoming* series does have a widespread, life-altering event, the trouble starts with smaller, localized situations. Things that, on their own, would not be world changing. Things that could easily be prepared for.

While I do offer preparedness tips in my stories, they are designed to be fun fiction, a way for you to start thinking about the "what ifs" that could happen while entertaining. When my first books came out, a few months prior to the pandemic, I received a rather scathing review. The reviewer's main issue: the characters in my story went to the store and bought toilet paper and paper towels. Hmmm...

Preparedness is Not a New Idea

Preppers and preparedness may be buzzwords of recent years, but the concepts aren't new. One of my favorite books, *Letters of a Woman Homesteader* by Elinore Pruitt Stewart, is a collection of letters from 1909 to 1914. In a few of the letters, she details how she grew her garden and tended her homestead to have a year's worth of food.

Mrs. Stewart was the norm. Our just-in-time system of having a grocery store at our whim is a new concept. Many times, communities banded together. Some farmers may have grown the cereal crops, a few ranchers harvested the beef, etc.

Obviously, we live quite differently now, with more people in cities than in rural areas. Even so, helping others is another reason to prep. Preparedness strengthens communities. Like in days past, some in the community may grow gardens, others may be amateur radio aficionados, yet others trained for medical emergencies.

Storing Water

In the previous chapter, I shared how we started our emergency preparedness journey after a windstorm took out our power for a week. That same windstorm left a neighboring town without water. When we started our preparedness efforts, that town without water was fresh in my mind.

Water is an excellent place to start. The recommendation of one gallon of water per person, per day for three days was common. Now the websites, like ready.gov and FEMA, which used to have the three-day recommendation, are changing their tunes.

Ready.gov now says one gallon per person for "several days" and FEMA says "consider" one gallon per person, per day for two weeks.

One gallon per day is truly the bare minimum each person needs when accounting for not only drinking but also hygiene.

But what about cooking? What if it's hot and you're sweating?

For three years we lived off the grid without running water. All of our water was brought in by using a handpump or being taken from our rain barrels. We were frugal with our water.

Even with being frugal, we used more than one gallon per day. And that was on days when we didn't do any laundry or take baths! It was simply water for drinking, cooking, dishes, and flushing the toilet. It really adds up.

Try it for a day or two. Commit to using only water you have stored. You may be surprised how much you use.

But you have to start someplace, and one gallon per person, per day makes the math easy! How many people are in your home? That's how many gallons you need for each day. My family of three (living at home) needs three gallons. Easy-peasy.

How Many Days?

"Several" is a very vague amount, and I'm not sure why ready.gov changed to that. Maybe they realized three days isn't enough, but they didn't want to commit to an exact number. Two weeks, FEMA's number, makes sense. Using that number of two weeks continues to make our math easy. By multiplying three people by fourteen days, I know my family needs forty-two gallons of water.

Forty-two gallons is nothing to sneeze at. And water is… well, wet. And heavy. Each gallon weighs just over eight pounds. Each gallon also occupies a specific amount of space.

An easy way to store those forty-two gallons would be in a large rain barrel. With one fifty-five-gallon barrel, we have more than enough. The trouble with the large rain barrels is they are heavy! At 8.34 pounds per gallon, a full barrel comes in at just under 460 pounds! It needs to be kept someplace sturdy, and it's certainly not portable.

How to Store Water

While we do have fifty-five-gallon and larger barrels for our water harvesting system, our ready-use water is kept in smaller containers. We use a combination of five-gallon jugs, recycled juice containers, and purchased gallon water jugs.

You can also get stackable five-gallon jugs. These are great for space issues but have tremendously increased in price over the last couple of years. We found Coleman containers locally at a reasonable price that were marketed for camping. And Igloo has a six-gallon container that is an okay price. The camping ones aren't designed to stack, but they don't have a terribly large footprint.

There are also cheaper options for storing water. Family-sized juice containers or two-liter soda bottles make decent water storage containers. The plastic is a nice thickness. When we first started our water storage, I told just about everyone I knew that I was collecting these bottles. I even put out a notice on Freecycle. (Remember Freecycle? Is it still around?)

The bottles should be well cleaned and sanitized. While these small jugs are easy to accumulate and easy to fill, plus very portable, they do take up space. I've found very creative places to store my bottles. Every closet, nook, and cranny gives an opportunity to snuggle in a jug.

I write the date I'm putting the water into storage and rotate the water at six-ish month intervals, keeping the containers for no longer than eighteen months. That is the amount of time I'm comfortable with because of concerns the plastic will break down.

What About Store-Bought Water?

The thin one-gallon jugs that water is usually purchased in are not suitable for long-term storage. The plastic will degrade. Milk jugs are not suitable for that same reason and because of the milk proteins—it's nearly impossible to get those jugs clean enough.

I do still buy jugs of water, especially if they are thicker jugs, similar to juice containers, as well as individual water bottles. I know to use the thin jugs first, and instead of adding them to long-term storage, they're kept for times we need a jug of water in the car.

Cases of water are often on sale in my area. The cases are handy and stack nicely. They're easy to rotate by keeping a date on them. And while we prefer reusable water bottles, there are many times we'll grab from an open case while running out the door.

Non-food-grade containers should not be used to store drinking or cooking water. You may wish to use these for toilet flushing water and other things.

Keep in mind, you may need more water than one gallon per person for fourteen days. Know your options for additional water sources. Many people have a WaterBOB that they plan to put into action at the first indication there may be a pending water issue.

Or just plan to fill the tub. While the WaterBOB is an okay option, provided you have the notice needed, a regular bathtub might not be suitable for drinking water without treatment. How clean is your tub?

Other Water Sources to Keep in Mind

Your hot water heater. Unless it's an on-demand one, it likely stores thirty or more gallons.

Can you set up rain gutters and harvest water? We get a surprisingly large amount of water collection with even a small amount of rain.

Where are your nearby natural water sources? Do you have the supplies needed to purify the water?

Purifying Water

Safe drinking water is essential for survival. We've all heard you can go three days without water. While this may be true, after a full day without water, you'll start to have difficulties. You'll feel thirsty and sluggish, followed by extreme fatigue, confusion, organ failure, and, eventually, death. And not everyone has the same tolerance for dehydration. Some may experience severe symptoms quicker than others. Making sure you know how to purify water in any situation is imperative.

There was a time I didn't worry about purifying water. While out hiking in the beautiful mountains, I'd greedily slurp from the bubbling stream. Cool and delicious, it tasted amazing. It may have tasted amazing, but after one trip I got sick. I had giardia. Not fun! Now, no matter how inviting the stream or creek looks, I filter my water before drinking. You should too.

When You Might Need to Purify Water

There are many situations where you may need to purify water, some planned and some unexpected. As mentioned, this could be when you're hiking or camping. Or there may be an emergency at home with your water supply such as broken water lines, unsafe tap water, or not having any tap water available.

Should You Store Water for Emergencies?

Yes, the first thing you should focus on when you start prepping is water. It's recommended that you have one gallon of water per person, per day. Ready.gov suggests three days' worth of water; FEMA now recommends two weeks.

Water Storage Containers

Buying water already in containers is fine for short-term needs (so you have something instead of nothing), but the thin gallon jugs do not hold up for long-term storage.

In the past, I've collected large soda and juice containers (they're a thicker plastic), but I now prefer stackable five-gallon containers or larger water tanks. For backpacking, I rely on a platypus, plus using some of the purification methods below.

Don't ration water! Drink what your body needs each day, even if it is the last bit you have. Plan to find new water as opposed to taking only sips. If you are home, remember the water in your hot water heater and the back of the toilet (not the bowl).

Away from home, look for rivers and creeks, ponds, lakes, and puddles. If it rains, snows, sleets, or hails, devise a way to capture the precipitation. A tarp can become a "roof" by adding a slight angle and bringing the fabric to a V with a collection container set below the V. Snow and hail can be melted. Be aware that dry snow melts down to about a tenth of what you started with. Wet snow melts down anywhere from a quarter to a half of the original amount.

Ten Simple Ways to Purify Water

In times of crisis or outdoor adventures, having clean water isn't just important—it's absolutely crucial. Water is the foundation of life itself, and ensuring it's safe to drink is nonnegotiable for staying healthy and resilient, no matter what challenges you face. This chapter dives into a variety of trusted methods for purifying water, equipping you with the knowledge and tools to secure safe drinking water wherever you find yourself.

Boiling Water: Time-Tested Reliability

At the time of this writing, the current recommendations from the CDC are to bring water to a rolling boil for one minute. If you are above 6,500 feet in elevation, you need to boil for three minutes. Some sources say to boil for ten. Filter cloudy or dirty water first. Remember, this method requires a heat source and a suitable container, making it essential for both urban and wilderness settings.

The CDC cautions: Water that has fuel, toxic chemicals, or radioactive materials in it will not be made safe by boiling or disinfection. Use bottled water or a different source of water if you know or suspect that your water might be contaminated with fuel or toxic chemicals.

Bleach: Household Solution for Emergency Water Purification

In emergencies, household bleach can effectively purify large quantities of water. For bleach having a 5 to 9 percent concentration of sodium hypochlorite (the most common in the United States), add eight drops (a little less than 1/8 teaspoon) per gallon and let stand for at least thirty minutes, to allow the bleach to neutralize pathogens. (See the Resources section for info on other concentrations.)

Filtering cloudy or dirty water beforehand enhances effectiveness, making this method suitable for cooking and family consumption during crises.

Water Purification Tablets: Swift and Effective

For purifying larger quantities of water, especially when clarity is an issue, water purification tablets are invaluable. Following the instructions provided, these tablets eliminate harmful microorganisms, making water safe for cooking and family consumption. Their ease of use and shelf stability make them an excellent choice for emergency situations.

If using cloudy or dirty water, you'll want to filter it first. Let the water settle, then pour into a new container. Use a bandanna, T-shirt, or something similar as your filter.

Water Treatment Drops: Simple and Versatile

Similar to purification tablets but in liquid form, water treatment drops offer flexibility in treating larger volumes of water. Following the specified guidelines, these drops effectively neutralize harmful microorganisms, making water safe for various uses, including cooking and family needs. Their versatility and effectiveness in different water conditions make them a valuable addition to any emergency preparedness kit.

Gravity Water Filtration System: Ideal for Groups and Extended Outings

Perfect for group settings or extended outdoor stays, a gravity water filtration system provides a convenient way to purify larger quantities of water. This method employs gravity to filter out contaminants, ensuring a steady supply of clean drinking water without the need for constant monitoring. Popular among backpackers and campers, it combines efficiency with ease of use.

Water Purifier Bottle: Portable and Functional

A dual-purpose solution, water purifier bottles not only store water but also purify it on the go. While they may require some adjustment for first-time users, many find these bottles convenient for everyday use and emergency situations alike. Their compact design makes them a practical choice for ensuring clean drinking water in various environments.

LifeStraw (and Similar "Straw" Brands): A Portable Lifesaver

A popular item in emergency kits, the LifeStraw offers individual water purification in a compact, lightweight form. Ideal for get-home bags or bug-out bags, this straw allows you to drink directly from water sources, filtering out bacteria and protozoa.

Since the design of the straw is intended to be used right from a water source, it can be hard to store enough clean water for your group or for a longer trip. It can also be awkward to use. One way to make it a little easier is to scoop water from the source using a bowl, bucket, or something similar, and drink from the container.

Berkey Filter: Comprehensive Home Water Filtration

For long-term water purification at home, the Berkey filter system stands out. Utilizing black filters that remove pathogens and optional additional filters for fluoride and arsenic, it ensures clean drinking water for household use. Its robust design and comprehensive filtration capabilities make it a preferred choice for maintaining water quality in domestic settings.

That said, though I've used the Berkey system personally for over a dozen years, recent concerns regarding the filtering system have come to light. I'm currently exploring other options to replace the black filters. My research isn't complete, but I will share three names of other filters that I'm looking at so you can pursue these at your leisure: AlexaPure (sold by My Patriot Supply), ProOne, and Boroux.

DIY Filters: Resourceful Solutions in Dire Situations

When conventional methods are unavailable, DIY filters offer a practical alternative. Using materials like charcoal and sand or rocks and sand, these filters effectively remove contaminants from water, albeit with varying degrees of efficiency. While not as reliable as commercial systems, they can provide a crucial lifeline in emergencies. Research these in advance so you are prepared to build before you need it!

Solar Still: Harnessing Nature's Power

In extreme conditions where water sources are scarce or contaminated with substances like radiation or saltwater, a solar still can be a lifesaving tool. By utilizing solar energy to distill water, this method produces potable water from otherwise unsafe sources. However, its effectiveness can vary depending on geographic and environmental factors, necessitating prior testing and adaptation to local conditions. This is another item you should research and learn about before it is needed.

Preparedness through Diversity

Ensuring access to clean water in emergencies requires foresight and preparation. By incorporating a variety of water purification methods into your emergency plan, you can safeguard your health and well-being in diverse scenarios. Whether in urban settings or the wilderness, these methods provide essential tools for securing a reliable water supply, ensuring resilience in challenging circumstances.

Finances

You may not think about finances as part of preparedness. In my opinion, it's an essential component.

I'm a fan of Dave Ramsey. His *Financial Peace* and *Total Money Makeover* books were very eye-opening and are available at most libraries. And many churches hold Financial Peace Seminars.

Setting up a budget is the first step to controlling your finances. A budget gives you a plan for how your money will be spent. When starting a budget, it's important to plan the most essential items first. Ramsey calls this the Four Walls:

- Food
- Utilities
- Shelter
- Transportation

He also recommends creating a zero-based budget each month, accounting for each dollar coming in and going out. It can take a few months to get the budget sorted out, but once you do, you'll love the feeling of creating—and sticking to—a monthly budget.

Once the budget is written, Dave Ramsey uses the Baby Step concept. Baby Step One is to establish an emergency fund. This emergency fund is used only for... e*mergencies.*

Washing machine breaks? The emergency fund is activated.

When the water pump went out on our truck a few months ago, our emergency fund covered the repair bill.

We use the emergency fund instead of credit cards. There is a whole lot of comfort in knowing that money is available.

After the emergency fund, the plan is to get out of debt. And stay out! Being debt-free gives you a lot of choices. The way to become debt-free is different for everyone. Some people sell all their excess stuff and get rid of their car and buy a beater. Others work second jobs. There are a lot of options, but the bottom line is you must be committed to it.

Cash on Hand

With everything happening right now, I believe at least a portion of your emergency fund should be in cash. Let's face it, we're not earning enough in interest to warrant leaving it in the bank anyway!

Combine this with using the envelope method for your day-to-day expenses. The envelope system is withdrawing cash from the bank each pay period for your purchases. Groceries, gas, restaurants…each goes into its own envelope, and you use cash to purchase these items. With the way things are, having cash on hand is a good idea.

How to Afford Emergency Preparedness

When we started preparing, we put ten dollars a week toward extra purchases. It was slow going, but it was all we could do then. Over time, I used other methods to trim our budget, and any savings were put in the prepper fund.

One of my favorite books for saving money is *The Complete Tightwad Gazette: Promoting Thrift as a Viable Alternative Lifestyle.* If you can, get the book! You will learn so many tips and tricks. Also, my Homespun Oasis blog contains many articles on saving money on food.

The majority of us need to work our preparedness efforts into our current budget. While setting up a budget can be done in a matter of hours or days (it will need tweaking; it's not a one-and-done endeavor), it takes time to build an emergency fund and even longer to get out of debt. And then, once out of debt, staying out of debt takes determination and diligence.

With the way things are today, many people are feeling an urgency to build a stockpile of water, food, and more immediately. I get this! I feel the same urgency. Even with the world situation, I'd think long and hard before pulling out a credit card and buying preparedness items.

Instead, examine your budget with a fine-tooth comb and find places you can cut back. As you're doing this, keep your Four Walls in mind. Those are food, utilities, shelter, and transportation.

These four items should be accounted for in your budget before anything else.

Once you've budgeted your Four Walls, everything else gets added in.

These are the items you may or may not need. For us, when we started our preparedness efforts, we had little excess money. To find dollars to put toward prepping, we had to cut other things. The first thing we got rid of was our satellite TV. That eighty dollars a month went toward food storage. We also severely cut down on dining out and moved that money to preparedness.

If you are a drive-thru coffee fan, cutting back from a daily mocha to twice weekly could translate to twenty pounds of rice and ten pounds of beans each week! I know, I know. Everyone always suggests cutting the coffee first. It's low-hanging fruit.

While cutting down on drive-thru coffee, dining out, and getting rid of satellite helped us start our preparedness goals, we also had to be creative, especially considering we were working on getting out of debt in conjunction with preparedness.

For paying off debt, Dave Ramsey calls this Gazelle Intensity. Truthfully, Old Dave wouldn't be too happy with us for splitting our debt reduction with buying stuff. But it's what works for us and helps us sleep at night.

How We're Currently Budgeting

We are currently pausing excess debt payments and stockpiling cash while increasing certain storage items. Dave suggests doing this during big life events such as expecting a baby. Our debt is minimal, and making only the minimum payments makes sense during this time.

We're also not keeping our emergency fund in the bank. The three cents a month in interest we were earning wasn't a big enough enticement to not have cash at the ready. With the cost of groceries on the rise and the minimal amount of interest being paid, I'm not sure a savings account (beyond what we are comfortable with for emergencies) makes sense right now (for us. You should do what makes sense for you and your family). Putting that money toward food you know you will eat will probably give you a larger "earning" in the long run.

Tips for Finding Extra Money

Right now, it may be extremely difficult to find extra money. Fuel and groceries are at an all-time high, and everything feels like a mess. You may need to trim your budget just to afford your day-to-day expenses.

What else can you do? Can you get a second job? Sell your second (or third) car? Excess furniture? Outgrown clothes? That exercise bike in the corner gathering dust? Consider every option for putting cash in your hand. Use that cash not only to build your food storage but also for the ever-mounting expenses.

If you think you have nothing left to cut, check the Resources section for an article from The Prudent Homemaker for more ideas.

Personal Fitness

Fitness as part of emergency preparedness wasn't something I thought much about—not until my health took a terrible turn. For a much too long stretch, I was miserable. I was tired all the time, to the point I could barely get off the couch. I thought I had a long-lingering flu.

Turns out it was menopause. It was also a wake-up call. It took some time to get myself well enough to move from that couch, but once I did, I made fitness a priority.

Physical fitness is a widely overlooked aspect of emergency preparedness. It's so much easier to buy some supplies and gear and call it good. Ten years ago, there is no way I could've hauled any of that gear more than a block or two. And that might be stretching it!

I'm still not in the shape I'd like to be in, but I can now carry a fully loaded backpack for five miles—uphill. Increasing my physical health also had a positive effect on my mental health. With daily movement, I'm better equipped to handle life. When I shirk on my movement quota, I decline in many ways.

How is Fitness Part of Emergency Preparedness?

Most of our preparedness efforts are concentrated on localized events. But if there was a widespread, life-altering scenario, we may find ourselves needing a drastic increase in the things we do daily. Gardening, hauling water (again), splitting wood...these things require physical stamina.

The better condition I am in today, the better I'd be in those circumstances. Not perfect, nowhere near perfect, but better.

My fitness routine isn't fancy. I use an online class called Healthy Moving, which encourages daily movement and shows ways to work this into my life, as well as longer mat classes.

My goal is bending, stretching, and moving several times throughout the day. I even set alarms on my phone to remind me to get up and stretch! I also shoot for two fifteen- to thirty-minute mat classes per week.

My family also does martial arts two times per week, I walk daily, and we hike at least one time per week. For the past couple of years we've taken the annual 52 Hike Challenge to help motivate us to get out there.

Sometimes those hikes are on snowshoes. What a workout that is! Two miles often feels like five, especially if we're breaking trail. Cross-country skiing is another winter sport we love. During the summer, we take longer hikes or overnight backpacking trips.

For your fitness efforts, you might want to join a gym, do DVDs or online streaming classes, or just start walking. Walking while carrying a backpack with a little weight in it is a surprisingly good workout. Depending on your health and fitness level today, your changes may be slow. That's okay! Anything you can do to improve is beneficial.

If you have mobility issues, think about alternatives and ways to make things easier. My mom uses a walker. She is not likely to ever go backpacking with me, but she can do chair yoga and other movements to improve her health. That's just one example, but over the past year, she's lost sixty pounds! *Way to go, Mom!*

This is also a good time to mention, if you have medication you rely on each day, do what you can to keep a supply of these on reserve. It's also a good time to mention you should always consult your physician before embarking on a new fitness routine.

Food Storage

I bet you thought I'd never get to this! While getting your water together, putting your finances in order, and walking around the block, you should start on your food storage. Nothing fancy or elaborate is needed. Remember, we don't want to go into debt for this!

The easiest and least expensive way to build your food storage is by purchasing extra things you already buy. Instead of one jar of peanut butter, buy two. Instead of two packages of pasta, buy three.

Mark the purchase date on the extra purchases and stash them in your cupboard. Next time you need to buy peanut butter, buy three. Date them. Use one now and stash two for later.

By buying items you already eat and rotating your stock, you'll help reduce waste. We like to use the popular motto of *eat what you store, store what you eat.* And combine that with the first in, first out (FIFO) method.

Building Your Supply Quicker

While buying extra will help build your stores, it is a slow process. Combine this with stocking up whenever there's a sale. It's no secret food prices have been drastically increasing. Even so, sales can still be found. Rice, beans, pasta, canned tomatoes, and other canned vegetables tend to be a good buy.

One great way to keep track of grocery prices is with a price book. This book can help you become aware of prices in your area and which stores have the best prices. It also lets you easily see when there's a sale. You can make a price book—a simple record of items you regularly buy with the prices you find—out of a notebook. Or you can buy a premade book to help you get started and format your own for future.

How Much Food Should You Store?

Normally, I'd suggest you start building your pantry to have enough food on hand for three days, then move to three weeks. Keep adding to your stores, using the FIFO method to rotate until you have an amount you are comfortable with.

Now, with the cost of everything going up and shortages on certain things, combined with the troubles worldwide, I'd work to get thirty days of food as quickly as possible. Increase from there.

If you can buy certain things in bulk, such as beans and rice, that's usually the most economical option. We order big bags of beans, lentils, wheat, and corn from Azure Standard. I buy twenty-pound bags of white rice from Walmart.

When properly stored, these dry goods can last a decade or longer. We're currently eating wheat we bought in 2012. It was stored in mylar bags with oxygen absorbers, nestled in a five-gallon bucket. The wheat is still perfect! I even sprouted a batch a few days ago with excellent results.

If wheat (in its natural, raw form) is not a current part of your diet, you should learn how to use it before buying in massive bulk.

While many food calculators suggest storing four hundred pounds of grain per person for one year of food storage, this grain should be in a variety you are comfortable using or are willing to become comfortable using. You shouldn't stockpile four hundred pounds of wheat kernels if you have zero idea how to turn those into something edible.

Those four hundred pounds of grain can (and should) include a variety, such as wheat, rice, oats, pasta, barley, corn, and more.

Saving Money on Meat

Our most consistent savings over the years have been from buying in bulk and being willing to try "weird" things. For years, we kept the freezer full because many local farmers and ranchers knew we were the ones to call when they were doing home butchering and had parts they weren't fond of. One of my friends would call me up and say, "I've got a licker and a ticker for you."

We'd also get soup bones and amazing deals on other things. One dairy farmer offered us roasts and ground meat for 99¢ a pound! And we'd often get calls from people right before hunting season asking if we wanted to help them clean out their freezer. We'd do the same and give away chicken legs to anyone who wanted them.

Yes, these things are likely location-dependent, but you may have similar opportunities in your area. People may not offer you last year's antelope, but maybe there are fruit trees or fields for gleaning. Every dime shaved off your food budget each week can be put toward food storage and supplies.

Saving Money at the Grocery Store

Loss leaders (those items the grocery stores markdown to rock bottom prices to entice you in so you'll buy more of the non-sale items) are another great way to save. I'm not one to run to multiple grocery stores (we only have two in town!), but I will buy extras of things I know we'll use when they're on sale. I also plan meals specifically around perishable sale items.

These loss leaders tend to be seasonal. St. Patrick's Day means lower prices on cabbage and sometimes corned beef. Cans of tuna are often on sale during Lent. Eggs typically go down at Easter. Right now, we may not see the same items or the deep discounts, but it is still worth watching for these and purchasing accordingly.

For most people, the biggest grocery expense is meat. Meat is also the most expensive thing to add to your food storage. Cans of tuna★ are very popular for food storage. At fifty to seventy-five cents a can, they seem like a great buy. But how many of those little five-ounce cans do you need to make a meal? Doing the math might surprise you.

Salvage grocers may also be an option for bulk and/or rock bottom prices. These items are usually scratch-and-dent or near the end of the best-by date. Salvage store purchases may or may not be good choices for your food storage depending on the item and their best-by date.

The best-by date doesn't mean the food magically goes bad on that date, but it is a good indicator of when to use it by. Even if salvage goods aren't suitable for longer-term storage, they could help with opening up more room in your budget to buy other items.

★While I do buy tuna to keep on my shelf, it's not part of my long-term food storage. Tuna in water gets mushy. You may not mind this, but if you do, decide how much tuna is a reasonable amount to keep on hand and be sure to practice first in, first out. Tuna isn't the only item that's not well-suited for long-term storage. Anything containing high fat tends to go rancid. Things like crackers, while shelf-stable, go stale after time. Pay attention to these items and rotate them properly.

Buying in Bulk

One of our budgeting techniques is to reduce our weekly grocery spending as low as possible. We ate plain, simple meals while not only building our food storage but also switching to a traditional foods diet. On my blog, you can find years' worth of menu plans mostly focused on rice, beans, and wild game in an effort to eat nourishing and inexpensive food.

We found that buying our basic foods in bulk gave us the most bang for our buck. With grocery costs increasing, bulk is usually still a better deal pound for pound.

Around the time we decided to get serious with our preparedness efforts and really bulk up our food storage (see what I did there?), I read some preparedness tips on a survival forum, and one stated that the absolute least expensive way to get a year's supply of food was to buy four hundred pounds of whole dried corn, sixty pounds of whole peas, six pounds of table salt, and four gallons of vegetable oil.

While we preferred sea salt and coconut oil, the idea of dried corn and dried peas had merit. And when I checked the prices on Azure Standard (where I got most of my bulk items) peas were the least expensive legume and corn was the least expensive grain at that time.

Hesitation About Buying in Bulk

I'll admit, I was hesitant to buy in bulk. What if we bought a big bag of something and we hated it or I didn't know how to cook it? The easy solution: buy smaller amounts and make a few dishes to try it out.

Or what if we bought a lot and it went bad? Another easy solution: learn how to properly prepare for long-term food storage. Beans, rice, barley,

27

oats, corn, and more store for years in Mylar bags with oxygen absorbers tucked in a five-gallon bucket.

For some items, I use my vacuum sealer instead of Mylar and buckets. The vacuum sealer works great from things like pasta.

Preparedness Tips for Buying in Bulk

Even if it was the most economical, I didn't start with whole peas and dried corn. I started with things we were familiar with: pinto beans, black beans, rice (lots of rice), and a few others.

But soon I was having so much fun trying new things, we just continued. Buying wheat was fun! Hard red, hard white, soft white—I had no idea there were so many varieties or that each had a different flavor and special use.

I did finally get around to trying whole peas when another friend shared her whole pea sprouting adventures. Peas are very good and very cheap. Like everything, the price of whole peas has increased, but they are still less than my beloved pinto beans, black beans, and even lentils.

Buying in bulk, even with today's prices, can still save you money. There are other online websites to order in bulk, plus local health food stores or regular grocery chains may place bulk orders for you.

Don't limit yourself to giant twenty-five or fifty-pounds bags either. An eight-pound bag of pinto beans from your local store may be less per ounce than the one-pound bag or what you can order. Check the math for the best deal.

While we do package our bulk purchases for long-term storage, we still eat these items (store what you eat, eat what you store) and rotate these (first in, first out—or FIFO) just like the "regular" grocery store foods.

We also don't just rely on those bulk grains and legumes. We add in a substantial amount of sea salt, coconut oil, herbs, spices, and more. Many of these are also purchased in bulk.

Some grocery stores do case lot sales or special bulk buying events. I include these in bulk buying. This is when a price book really comes in handy. You can easily see if the case price of tomatoes beats what you can find on regular days.

Tip: Not only should you know how to cook, bake, or prepare everything in your food storage, but consider how you will do these things during a power outage or other event. Does your stove/oven work if the power is out? Do you have alternate cooking methods?

How to Package Food for Long-Term Storage

Would you like to ensure your long-term food storage is as fresh in a decade (or two) as it is today? Spending a little time and money today can guarantee those beans, grains, rice, and more are well protected. The secret? An oxygen-free environment.

Each summer, usually in June or early July, we do a pantry and cabinet cleanup and inventory. We go through not only our shelf-stable items but also our long-term food storage.

As we're checking our inventory, we often find the need to place new orders of bulk goods, like beans, grains, or rice. While the cheapest way to purchase these items is usually in bulk packaging, storing them in the same packaging is not the best way to keep them for the long term. Instead, you want to create an oxygen-free environment.

With proper storage—using Mylar bags, oxygen absorbers, and plastic buckets—beans, rice, and grains will last practically forever. Not long ago, I opened a five-gallon bucket of lentils from 2012, stored in Mylar with oxygen absorbers, and they are as fresh as a small bag we purchased a few months ago. Using a vacuum sealer is another great way to preserve some foods for the long term.

Mylar Bags

If you've researched long-term food storage, you've likely heard of Mylar. It's the most common "do it yourself" way to prepare items bought in bulk. Sure, you can purchase buckets and cans of already sealed grains, beans, rice, and much more, but usually, the convenience of already sealed items comes at a cost.

For the most part, it's cheaper to purchase items in bulk packaging, which usually arrives in plastic or paper bags. These bags are fine for short-term storage of a few weeks or maybe a month, but they aren't suitable for the long term.

By purchasing Mylar bags and oxygen absorbers (they often come together, but you can purchase them separately as well) and buckets with lids (or finding them for cheap or free), you can quickly and easily transform those plastic bags into long-term food storage solutions.

Okay, great. But…

What Exactly is a Mylar Bag?

Mylar's a trademark from DuPont for a polyester film made from stretched polyethylene terephthalate (PET). Mylar has high strength, is resistant to extreme temperatures, and provides a barrier to moisture, light, gas, and odors. These characteristics make it very popular for food storage. Mylar is also used in emergency blankets.

Since Mylar is a brand name, you may find food storage bags that look like Mylar but go by a different name, such as Metalized Storage Bag or Dry Pack Pouch. This is fine, as long as what you have sourced is food grade.

Mylar (and the other brands) are available in a variety of thicknesses. When shopping for long-term food storage bags, you want a minimum thickness of three millimeters. If I know I'm going to store something with potentially sharp edges, such as pasta, I look for a higher thickness of around six millimeters or use an alternate storage method, such as a vacuum sealer.

These bags are available in a variety of sizes and are great for storing small items in metalized pouches to large five-gallon sizes. For most of our food storage, we use the five-gallon ones, but the one-gallon is also useful. Small bags are also wonderful to use for things like spices or individual packages of nuts or seeds for bug-out bags, get-home bags, and so forth.

Going hand in hand with the Mylar bags are oxygen absorbers.

What Are Oxygen Absorbers?

Oxygen absorbers are little packets designed to remove oxygen from a sealed environment. They help maintain food quality, protect from insects, and extend shelf life for long-term food storage.

The oxygen absorber packets are made from a porous material and filled with an iron powder that becomes iron oxide in the presence of oxygen. The way the packets are made allows the oxygen and moisture to enter, but the iron powder doesn't leak out, making it safe to use for food.

When you purchase oxygen absorbers, they'll arrive sealed. Most oxygen absorbers include a color indicator to show if the absorber is still good and ready to use. Once you open the container, they begin to work immediately, and you may notice they become warm to the touch.

After you open your package of absorbers, you'll want to move quickly to get all of them either added to the food package or put in a small glass mason jar sealed with a flat and a lid. After a few minutes or so, you may hear the jar pop as the oxygen is sucked out and the lid seals.

Once the oxygen has been removed, the chemical reaction stops. We have many Mylar bags that had oxygen absorbers added a decade or more ago, and the bags are still tight and lack oxygen. That's what you want!

It's important to choose the right size of oxygen absorber for the size of Mylar bag. When buying bags and oxygen absorbers as a package deal, they'll usually come in the correct size. One-gallon bags need 300 to 600cc absorbers, and five-gallon bags need 2,000 to 3,000cc absorbers.

What Foods to Use Oxygen Absorbers With

Also important is to know which foods to package in Mylar bags with oxygen absorbers and which foods not to. You should only use oxygen absorbers with dry foods, such as wheat kernels, beans, corn, barley, etc. Anything with a moisture level over 10 percent is not safe to use with an oxygen absorber. You wouldn't use oxygen absorbers for powdered foods, like salt, baking soda, or sugar. This could cause a chemical reaction and/or turn the powder into a brick.

Some sources don't recommend using oxygen absorbers with brown rice or nuts because they have a high oil content and aren't suitable for long-term food storage. True...but I still package both of these items, knowing I won't get twenty years out of them but may get three, four, or five. Be sure to use First In, First Out (FIFO) for these types of items.

Some people may try to substitute Diatomaceous Earth and/or bay leaves for oxygen absorbers. While both of these are known to help with pests, they don't remove the oxygen. For long-term food storage of ten, twenty, or thirty years, you will want to use the oxygen absorbers.

How to Package Long-Term Food Storage Using Mylar

Gather Your Supplies:

- Buckets with lids (one-gallon, three-gallon, or five-gallon)
- Mylar bags (in sizes to match the buckets, or use several smaller bags in one large bucket)
- Oxygen absorbers

- A clothing iron and a piece of two-by-four or a flat board, OR a hair straightener
- A friend

This job is possible to do on your own, but it goes much easier with a friend, especially when hefting twenty-five or fifty-pound bags. You can purchase food-grade buckets, or you may be able to find them for cheap or free at a bakery. When we first started packaging our own long-term food storage, it was easy to get buckets for a dollar or less each. Now it's more challenging! But it's still worth asking around locally.

Another thing I like to have to go with my buckets is a bucket opener tool. This makes popping the lids off so much easier! You could also consider gamma lids. These can make opening the buckets easier, but for the cost, I'll stick with my less-than-four-dollar opener.

Get Everything Set Up

I like to set everything up before opening any bags, especially oxygen absorbers.

- Line up or stack the food items you're packaging
- Line up your buckets and have the lids nearby
- If using a Mylar bag the same size as the bucket, line the bucket with the bag; if using smaller bags, with a plan to store several in a bucket, lay them out so they are ready
- Heat up your iron or hair straightener
- Have a knife or scissors ready (to open packages)
- Have a mason jar with a flat and lid ready for the unused oxygen absorbers, or plan on resealing the packaging with your iron/hair straightener
- Take a look around…is everything ready?
- If you have everything, let's go!

Now Fill Your Bags

One person holds the bag and/or bucket while the other person pours. Make sure you leave headroom at the top. The contents should end a few inches below the top of the bucket. Shake down the contents and add more if needed. Label the bag with the contents.

Once all your containers are filled, you can open the oxygen absorbers. Take out only the amount you need. I like to buy smaller oxygen absorber packages that have five inside so I'm only working with five at a time. This number feels manageable to me. Any additional oxygen absorbers that you aren't using immediately need to be put in the mason jar and sealed, or reseal the packaging using the iron/hair straightener.

Working quickly, same as the oxygen absorbers are doing, you want to get everything sealed. Manually push on the bag to remove as much air as possible.

If using an iron and board, lay the board on one side of the bag and the iron on the other, at the top of the bag. (Here's where you need your friend again.) Start in the center to make a seal, then seal one end and then the other. With the open spaces still available, push down on the bag again to remove more air before sealing the entire top.

If you're using a hair straightener, use the same process of starting at the center and then sealing both ends, removing more air before finishing the seal.

What to do After the Bags are Sealed

Once sealed, tuck the bag into the bucket and check for a tight seal to ensure no air is escaping. If there's air, check your seal and fix the problem. Once all is good, push all the Mylar down into the bucket and put the lid on.

I then add a piece of masking tape to the top and a second piece on the side, large enough to write the bucket contents and date on. You may also wish to add how many pounds are in the bucket. My process for smaller Mylar packages or vacuum-sealed ones is much the same. I label the container they're stored in (usually a five-gallon bucket) with the contents and date. I note how many packages there are and the approximate package size.

Once it's labeled in both places, double-check that the lid is on tight and then set it aside.

The oxygen absorbers take up to four hours to fully absorb all the oxygen. I like to check the bucket after that to make sure everything is tightly sealed. If I have any doubt, I'll unseal and try again. If it's good, I move them to a staging area and check in a week. If all is well, it's then moved to my long-term food storage area.

When all the bags/buckets are sealed, pour yourself a cup of tea and put your feet up! Take this opportunity to add your buckets to your spreadsheet, too, if this is part of your process.

How to Package Long-Term Food Storage Using a Vacuum Sealer

For some items, such as high-moisture things like almond or coconut flour, I use a vacuum sealer instead of Mylar and oxygen absorbers. While I do buy some vacuum seal bags, I prefer the rolls so I can make my own size of bags. These come in handy for small items like spices or larger items like spaghetti.

Note: Consider exactly what you are vacuum sealing. Sharp objects can poke a hole in the bag. I've had good results with things like spaghetti and coconut flakes, but not everyone does. For these questionable items, you may wish to stick with the stronger, thicker Mylar.

There are many varieties of vacuum sealers. You'll want to follow the instructions included with your device. If you're shopping for a vacuum sealer, look for one that has an optional jar attachment port. These allow you to suck the air out of a jar and are wonderful for things like home-dehydrated fruits and vegetables. I like to keep a large supply of mason jars on hand, so it makes sense to keep them filled instead of storing them empty, especially when working with limited storage space.

Maintenance of Your Long-Term Food Storage

I check all my Mylar bags one time per year, when we do our pantry cleaning and organization, to ensure the seals are still tight and all is well. I don't open the Mylar packaging until I'm ready to use the contents. If I do use the contents, I'll just take out a portion (enough to fill a gallon-size glass jar) and then reseal the Mylar. When resealing, you must add new oxygen absorbers.

Recordkeeping

Part of my plan also includes keeping a spreadsheet and updating it as needed (when things are used or more product is added). At the annual pantry cleaning, the spreadsheet is also checked for accuracy. Because I don't have one area with enough space for all of my pantry and long-term food storage, I also note on the spreadsheet where things are located. It's a good system and is very helpful when I'm looking for that bucket of lentils that needs opened next.

Heat and Eat Bin

For many years, the "official recommendation" from most state and federal agencies was to keep three days of food on hand at all times. In the last ten years or so, following longer-term power outages and other issues, many agencies have upped that recommendation to one to two weeks. I appreciate these extended recommendations and suggest you ear mark this emergency food and keep it in a separate location.

I told you about our real-life experience of being without power for several days during the Great Coastal Gale. Not only were we without power, but our entire county was also without power. The grocery stores were either closed or extremely limited. Restaurants were closed. Even gas stations were closed or limiting fuel.

The house we lived in was entirely electric. When the power went out, our ability to cook also went out. We were blessed to have a camp trailer with a stove/oven, plus a small camp stove. With our cooking options being outside of our home, quick-to-prepare items were very helpful. At that time, we ate a Standard American Diet, consisting of mainly boxed and canned goods, allowing us plenty of quick meals.

These days, most of the food we eat is prepared from scratch, and a good portion of it requires extensive cooking times. Because I want foods on hand for emergency needs, we created a Heat and Eat Bin. And, because of our experiences, we've never kept just a three-day supply. Because of our own experiences, we now have two heat and eat bins each holding seven days' worth of foods and essentials, giving us a full two weeks.

It is important to remember that canned food overall has less nutrition than fresh food. Many real food enthusiasts choose to never eat food from a can. In day-to-day life, we limit the amount of processed foods we have in our diet. But in an emergency situation, things could rapidly change.

For us, this truly is a bin. I use a large Rubbermaid-style container. In this bin are foods that require no preparation other than opening up the can or jar, adding water to rehydrate, and then possibly heating up. The foods in this bin are "convenience" style foods, as opposed to foods we eat daily. Keeping them in the bin separates them from the standard kitchen fare, designating them as "special."

While these are convenience foods, they are foods that I purchased after scouring the ingredient list and deciding they were okay for the intended purposes. The intended purpose: emergency use.

Another great thing about having the bin is that it is portable. If we were ever in a situation where we needed to leave home in a hurry, we could grab our Heat and Eat Bin and our camping bin (which happen to be conveniently located right next to each other). Besides the bin with a week's worth of food and essentials, a bug-out bag is also a good idea, which we'll talk about in a later chapter.

The Heat and Eat Bin can also be quite convenient for times when I'm under the weather and someone else is cooking. While the bin foods are okay, they are certainly not as tasty as the foods we prepare ourselves. Originally, I thought the children might be tempted to open a can of soup as a snack (that is part of the reason for stashing them in a bin). I still vividly remember the time my daughter, then in her early teens, opened a can of soup and declared it to not taste as good as she expected. She didn't go as far as saying my cooking is better, but it was still nice to hear.

What's in the Bin?

I'm so glad you asked! This is a general list and does change based on any good deals I may find:

- Salmon
- Sardines
- Tuna
- Black beans (canned)
- Pinto beans (canned)
- Greens (canned; read labels, some contain MSG)
- Assorted soups (the kinds that don't need water added)
- Instant oatmeal/grits packets (do you have water stored?)
- Granola bars/snack bars/meal bars
- Nuts, seeds, and raisins
- Dehydrated backpacking meals (needs water)
- Water (several individual bottles in addition to my regular water storage)
- Water purifying tablets
- Can opener (my husband likes the P 38 style, but I prefer something beefier)
- Backpacking stove, fuel, cook pot, headlamp

To add a homemade element, I also do my own dehydrating. I love the ideas from Backpacking Chef, and my friend Wardee from Traditional Cooking School has an eCourse all about dehydrating. I should note, I've tried to keep jerky in our Heat and Eat Bin and in our bug-out bags, but it seems to disappear! If you can keep it from walking off, jerky is a great option.

First In, First Out

Just like with all food storage, it is important to rotate these items. Since our bin contains things we do not eat regularly, I make sure to check it each year when I do my pantry clean out.

When adding to the bin, I mark the date on each item with a Sharpie. Not the expiration date, but the date I purchased it. I check this first then check the expiration date provided by the manufacturer.

Anything that will expire before the following year's check gets pulled and added to our regular menu. New items are purchased for the bin on the next shopping trip. While these expiration dates are not the date the product is no longer safe to use, it just makes sense to us to keep things current.

Also in the bin are miscellaneous items like a can opener, disposable dishes and silverware, salt, pepper, a roll of toilet paper, paper towels, and a sturdy jug of water. These things are there specifically in the case of taking the bin and going.

Do you need a Heat and Eat Bin?

Maybe or maybe not. You may choose to keep only three days of emergency food in your bug-out bag and anything additional is simply in your cabinets or on your shelves. The important thing to remember is to stock foods you and your family will enjoy but are also convenient.

Easy No-Cook Meals and Food Storage Items

Prepping isn't just relegated to end-of-the-world scenarios. Preparation for not only weather events specific to your area but things like unemployment and illness is smart. Imagine how wonderful it would be to know you have a pantry full of food if you suddenly find yourself out of work. That said, I believe it's smart to consider society-changing scenarios when planning for an unknown future.

Guerilla Eats

In addition to regular long-term storage foods, such as beans, grains, and freeze-dried items, have you considered guerilla eating? In my early days of preparedness, a good friend, who was a longtime prepper, shared with me her stealthy—or guerilla—food plans. I suspect many of us have heard of guerrilla gardening, which is essentially planting hidden caches of food and the idea of keeping rabbits for protein because they're quiet and don't require much space.

But have you thought about the foods in your storage? And have you thought about the odors those foods will give off while you cook?

My friend did! She focused much of their food storage on ready-to-eat items, no cooking required. I love the idea and added many of her suggestions to my own pantry.

No-Cook Ideas

There's a multitude of no-cook or quick-cooking, low-odor foods available. I've compiled a list of a few that we store, shelf life, and some suggestions for no-cook meals. This is just the tip of the iceberg, and you'll be able to add plenty of personal favorites. For more ideas, be sure to read my book *No-Cook Meals for Your Food Storage.*

Nuts and Nut Butters

These are a great addition for short-term food storage but don't have the stability of keeping for years and years. Depending on the variety of nuts, expect less than a year when storing them in your pantry.

Nuts still in the shell and/or stored in the freezer will keep longer. We buy raw nuts in bulk from Azure Standard to vacuum seal, then keep them in a cool, dark location. We add in containers of roasted peanuts or mixes when we find a good deal on them. Sunflower, sesame, and pumpkin seeds are also good items to consider.

The oil in nut butters can go rancid, but commercial peanut or almond butter have a shelf life of about two years when unopened. I've stretched this to three years by keeping in a cool, dark closet. It may go past that date, but that's when we use it.

If you buy natural peanut butter, without preservatives, these have a shorter shelf life. Use the best-buy date on the jars but figure on it being good for another six to eight months.

SunButter, or sunflower seed butter, is another option. The shelf life on this is officially about a year. Extend this with proper storage (cool and dark).

Dried Fruit

Like nuts, dried fruit is a great ready-to-eat option. Combining dried fruit and nuts makes a handy trail mix. We keep a variety of dried fruit on hand, including raisins, apricots, figs, dates, and coconut (both chips and shreds).

Depending on the fruit, the shelf life is anywhere from a year (again, when unopened and properly stored, this can just about double) to a decade. We've had unsweetened coconut shreds and chips vacuum-sealed since 2012. I opened a package a few weeks ago that is still as fresh as the day it was purchased!

Nuts and dried fruits not only make a great trail mix but also a snack bar when whirred in a food processor.

We have a solar system that gives us electricity even if the grid is down. (Unless there's an EMP. In that case, will the solar system survive the pulse? A question that doesn't seem to have a definite answer...) But having a manual food processor is still a good idea. I've found soaking the nuts and seeds in water before processing makes the process go easier. It'll still take a little elbow grease but nothing like starting with unsoaked raw nuts.

Bonus! Soaking raw nuts makes them more digestible.

Lentils

Now we're talking! With proper packaging (Mylar bags with oxygen absorbers stored in a sealed bucket), lentils will keep for a couple of decades. Sprouted lentils do not require cooking before eating.

A long twenty-four-hour soak and several days of sprouting make lentils perfectly edible. Add a little olive oil, balsamic vinegar, salt, and pepper for a fabulous no-cook salad. This is so easy to make, I often bring along a sprouting bag to sprout lentils for a salad while traveling!

I share my love of lentils and favorite preparation methods in my book *Stretchy Beans: Nutritious & Economical Meals the Easy Way* and how lentils work in our travel plans in *Real Food Hits the Road*. And be sure to grab my book *Sprouts for Your Food Storage* to learn how to sprout lentils.

Quinoa

Once considered peasant food, quinoa has developed a reputation in recent years as a superfood due to being a high-protein plant food. Most resources I find show quinoa, a seed commonly referred to as a grain or pseudo-grain, with a shelf life of three years. Again, my own experience with airtight storage has proven much beyond that.

Like lentils, I soak and sprout quinoa, making it ready to eat. I've found older quinoa doesn't sprout as well as fresh quinoa, but it still develops small tails and is wonderfully soft and edible. When sprouting, be sure to taste your sprouts at each rinsing to get the taste you prefer.

The nutritional profile of soaked and sprouted quinoa is similar to cooked, coming in at 222 calories, 39 grams of carbs, 4 grams of fat, 8 grams of protein, and 5 grams of fiber per cup. Quinoa is also naturally gluten-free. Quinoa is another one of my favorite travel foods.

Check out *Real Food Hits the Road* for more info on how we eat away from home. And also grab *Sprouts for Your Food Storage* to learn all about sprouting quinoa.

Chia Seeds

These powerful little gems have a mild flavor, tending to take on whatever they're mixed with. When added to water, they plump up into a gelatinous pudding-like dish and make a great egg substitute. I'm not overly fond of chia seeds because they stick in my teeth, but their nutritional profile is hard to beat.

Despite their tiny size, chia seeds are one of the most nutritious foods on the planet. They're loaded with fiber, protein, omega-3 fatty acids, and various micronutrients. And yes, they are the same seeds that are loved for growing "hair" on Chia Pets.

Other Grains, Seeds, and Legumes

Many grains, seeds, and legumes* lend themselves to no-cook eating. My favorite guerilla method…sprouting!

Sprouting radish, broccoli, and alfalfa seeds is a great way to add greens to your diet. I love sprouting during the dark days of our long Wyoming winter to help ease the strain on our grocery budget.

Sprouting is inexpensive and doesn't require fancy equipment. When sprouting beans or large grains like wheat, my favorite device is a colander. For small seeds, such as radish, I like to use a simple sprouting lid that screws onto a wide-mouth mason jar. I've also used an old piece of pantyhose instead of a special lid with fine results!

You can also let your sprouts grow out to become microgreens. Sprouting wheat, spelt, farrow, or einkorn takes several days to develop tails and when finished still tend to be a little too al dente to eat raw. However, growing out these cereal grains into microgreens gives them the ability to become no-cook food. Microgreens take about two weeks until they're ready to eat.

Oats, both rolled and quick-cooking, are fabulous for food storage and no-cook meals. Their shelf life, when stored in Mylar or vacuum-sealed, is many years. They provide healthy carbs, lots of fiber, and even some protein.

Soak rolled oats overnight for a cold breakfast cereal. Quick-cooking oats only need a few hours of soaking until they're ready to eat. You can even use oats in no-bake/no-cook snack bars.

*Important note: not all beans and legumes are safe to eat raw. Example: You must boil and cook kidney beans to remove toxicity.

Whey Protein Powder

This is an easy just-add-water food storage option and also makes simple no-cook meals. The shelf life for these powders is only one or two years, depending on the brand. You'll want to practice the "first in, first out" method and use whey protein powder in your daily life to make it realistic.

Be sure to check the ingredients when choosing your whey protein powder; many are heavily processed. Once you find a brand you're happy with, consider purchasing it in plain and flavored varieties. Add whey protein powder to oatmeal or rice to increase the protein content, blend into homemade snack bars (see dried fruit above) or add to simple protein balls. Another good option are these whey protein bars from Naken Nutrition.

Collagen and/or Gelatin

While not the same, collagen and gelatin are similar enough to list together. Here's a helpful quote about the similarities:

"Collagen peptides are simply amino acids of gelatin broken down into smaller molecules through a natural process. The main difference between the two is that collagen is more therapeutic and they also act a little differently in the kitchen. Gelatin gels when cooled after being mixed with liquids (think jiggly jello) while collagen does not. Some of the studies cited here may use the simple term 'collagen' or use other names for it like 'hydrolyzed collagen' or 'collagen peptides.' These are all different names for the same thing." (From Trim Healthy Mama)

Collagen or gelatin mixed in warm water or tea can add much-needed protein. Either make a great addition to oatmeal, no-cook snack bars, protein bars, and more. Be sure to check the Resources section for a yummy Creamy Rice recipe—one of my favorite ways to make both gelatin and collagen part of our regular diet.

Gelatin and collagen have a fairly long shelf life. While the recommendation for most brands is one year, I've used collagen that is more than five years old. The taste was fine, but I do wonder if the nutritional profile changed.

Like whey protein powder, use this in your daily life to help it make sense as part of your food storage program. Stronger nails and shiny hair are a bonus to adding these to your diet! There's even some research showing collagen and gelatin can help you feel full and aid in weight loss while increasing brain function.

Canned Fruit, Vegetables, Fish, and More

We know that many canned goods, a staple in most kitchens, are easily opened and enjoyed. (Tip: make sure you have a manual can opener or two.)

I like to stock fruits, tomatoes (yes, I know, I know…it's a fruit), tuna, salmon, sardines, (you will have odor with canned fish but less than cooking odors), coconut milk, and more. Ready-to-eat soups, baked beans, and canned beans don't require heating. The flavor profile is less than when heated, but they'll still fill your stomach and make easy no-cook meals.

Other items to consider include nori sheets (great stuffed with tuna or sardines and radish sprouts), thin rice noodles (soak until soft and then top with baked beans), rice paper (thirty seconds in hot water turn these into a great wrap), and bulgur or couscous along with "instant" rice can be soaked until soft and used as a base or salad.

We often take instant rice flakes on backpacking trips. Put the rice flakes in a soaking container after breakfast (an empty, clean, lidded peanut butter jar works great) along with dehydrated refried beans. By the time we're ready for lunch, it's a soft spread ready to fill a tortilla. So good!

The grain version of instant rice (Minute Rice) takes longer to soften when using cold water but only takes five minutes with hot water.

And instant refried beans are a flavorful no-cook meal idea. When we're getting ready for a backpacking trip, we make our own (cook, drain, puree, then dehydrate beans) but also keep a few different store-bought varieties in our pantry.

A few times a year, I dehydrate other no-cook goods such as jerky (both strips and ground meat style), potato bark, yogurt bark, and complete meals.

Dehydrating my own no-cook meals gives me the advantage of knowing exactly what's in them. They have a shelf life of about a year (when properly dried and stored airtight) and give us great variety for hiking, backpacking, and more food storage security. Some, in the case of jerky and yogurt bark, don't even require water to eat.

Freeze-Dried and Ready-Made Snacks

While the bulk of our food storage consists of common everyday items with a long shelf life, we do keep a small assortment of freeze-dried items on hand. Most of these are in #10 cans and are individual items as opposed to meals, things like freeze-dried chicken, black bean burger, corn, strawberries (and other fruit), and the like.

Many of these freeze-dried items can be eaten as is. Freeze-dried fruit makes a tasty snack, and freeze-dried corn is a little like corn nuts. (These are a great addition to the rice and bean rollups mentioned above. Adding a bit of crunch makes the rollups really sing). These freeze-dried items are convenient and have a super long shelf life.

But this does come at a cost. We've chosen to add these in small amounts, concentrating our food storage money on less expensive items.

Commercial snack foods, such as granola bars, breakfast bars, and crackers, are other no-cook options. These, too, have a higher cost per ounce than many other options and the shelf life is limited. While we do keep these on hand, they're a part of our everyday foods—quick snacks to grab on the way out the door—as opposed to food storage items.

Food Storage Takes Time

Please don't get discouraged thinking you'll never have all the food storage you should. It takes time to build it up. Make the effort to put as much aside as you can. Don't go into debt to do it, but consider making other sacrifices. Instead of going out for a burger and fries, can you eat at home and buy the difference in rice and beans?

I also don't suggest buying all of one food category at one time. It might be tempting to buy four hundred pounds of wheat and be done with the grain category, but what will you eat with that wheat?

Theoretically, you may be able to have wheat at breakfast, lunch, and dinner, but should you? Would you get all the nutrients you'd need? And how long would it take before you couldn't stand the sight of another bowl of wheat porridge?

We need variety in our diet. And we need spice! Salt, too, for that matter. Buying extras of things you normally buy, while adding in select bulk items, will give you a well-rounded variety.

If you need a little more guidance, you could consider making a three-day menu plan of easy-to-cook items (spaghetti and sauce, rice and beans, oatmeal, etc.). Use this menu plan to stock up your three days of goods.

And make sure you have a manual can opener and at least one alternative-cooking method. Also, keep in mind that a stove that runs on gas or propane may have safety features that prevent the oven from working if the power is out.

Emergency Kits

Everyday Carry Bag (EDC)

There are certain things I remember about my Grandpa Dick. He always wore a gray button shirt with a pocket and a pocketed T-shirt underneath. He wore black working boots, slip-on cowboy style, that went to the middle of his calf. Grandpa Dick was a blue-collar worker, in charge of the grain co-op in the small Kansas town where we lived when I was a child.

My grandpa died when I was thirteen. Even having only those few short years with him, many of his mannerisms and habits were ingrained in me. He was the first person I knew who practiced Everyday Carry. Oh, he didn't call it that, of course. I'm not even sure EDC was a thing back in those days.

He always had specific things in his pockets: a pocketknife, a refillable lighter, and a handkerchief. Every. Single. Day. He never left home without these things.

What is EDC?

You might be wondering what's this Everyday Carry thing is, commonly referred to as EDC in preparedness circles. Is it just stuffing your purse or pockets with things you might need?

Yeah. Pretty much.

My grandpa carried those three things every day because he had a need for them. I can't tell you how many times he pulled out that pocketknife and made use of it. I never saw him use Kleenex, just the handkerchief. And the lighter…did I mention the shirt pocket had a pack of smokes in it? Yes, he knew they were bad for him. Believe me, I made sure he knew it.

Just a Purse?

When I started thinking about my own purse as more than a cute handbag and the vehicle to carry things I couldn't imagine leaving home without, I realized this was another similarity I had with my grandpa.

EDC isn't something I focused on until a few years ago. Back in the day, when I had an office job, I had a collection of purses which coordinated with my outfits. Other than moving the wallet into the purse of the day, I rarely thought about other things I might need.

Twenty-some years ago, I watched a "Mad About You" episode where Jamie accidentally switched purses with her sister. Jamie, always organized and together, had a purse with just about anything in it you could imagine. Things to help her always look pulled together. Her sister, not so much. Throughout the episode, it showed how Jamie's day fell apart without her own bag, and her sister's day came up roses. The power of the Everyday Carry!

My EDC Bag

Gone are the days of a purse to match my every outfit. When I began working from home many years ago, I discovered I only need one handbag for everyday and a second I keep in the closet for those rare times I dress up.

I had a super simple black cross-body bag. It served me well for years, and I loved it. The cross-body part is important for me so I can carry it securely and hands-free. It also helps me not leave it somewhere. I can't tell you how many times I've left my purse in a restaurant or at a friend's home. Having it attached to my body is a huge help!

When it was time for a new bag, I stuck with the cross-body but went with something slightly larger. I'm not the type to carry a purse that looks more like an overnight bag, but do need to have room for my day-to-day essentials.

I'll admit, it took me several months before I found what I wanted. I finally settled on a Kavu bag. I picked out a fun pattern, shocking my adult children who were used to my standard black, and absolutely love the way the bag hangs. It's super comfortable and carries just the right amount. Not too large, but big enough I was able to add a few things I felt were missing from my old purse.

What's in the Bag?

Of course, I carry the normal stuff: my wallet containing my license, insurance card, debit card, and a few other things. For a wallet, I highly recommend a RFID blocking wallet or adding a blocking card to your current wallet.

I also carry cash. Even in today's world of easy-to-use plastic, cash is still king. For years, we've done some sort of envelope system via Dave Ramsey. Paying cash for groceries and fuel really helps control the budget. But this cash is not part of the envelope system, it's for unexpected needs; emergencies, if you will. How much emergency cash do you need? Only you can determine this. The amount I'm comfortable with may be way different than the amount you are comfortable with.

Depending on where you live, you might also keep a blank check in your wallet. There are still many, many places in my area accepting checks. One example, the tow truck driver. The last company we used gave us a discount for paying with a check instead of our credit card. Something to consider for your location also.

My cellphone and a small Swiss Army knife are part of my EDC. My Swiss Army has a light on it doubling as a flashlight. Plus, my cellphone has a flashlight. I used to carry a penlight, and may add that again in the future. Often times, I also have my Kindle, if I think I may have time for a good book while away from home.

A small first aid kit, of sorts, is also part of my EDC. I got a great burlap bag as part of an order from MadeOn: Skin Care Products. The little bag is the perfect size for my purse and easily holds a few band-aids, a MadeOn lip balm, hard lotion, a small container of analgesic, a ring of elastic (an excellent rubber band, compliments of my LuLaRoe lady), a couple of handy wipes, a make-up remover packet, and a handkerchief—just like Grandpa!

A few other miscellaneous items include a small notebook, pen, a small mirror (is there something in my teeth?), a comb, a second hard lotion (this one is scented and can double as an emergency deodorant after a quick use of the handy wipe), and Listerine strips.

What Else?

That's about it for my small bag. If you have a larger purse, backpack, specialty EDC pouch, a mini pocket-sized EDC pouch, or something similar, there may be other things you'd wish to consider. Maybe you need an umbrella as part of your EDC, a tablet (as opposed to a simple eReader), a folding knife, or a full make-up kit. The idea is to create an EDC perfect for you and your lifestyle. The perfect EDC likely won't happen on your first try.

Car Kit

Every vehicle should have an emergency kit. Your car might not start, you may get stuck, or you could even slide off the road. Your car kit could help you get back on the road quickly. It could also help save your life. Even if you always carry a get-home bag, a car kit contains additional, specialized, car-related items along with some overlap.

You could get a basic prebuilt emergency car kit that contains jumper cables (essential), emergency triangles or flares, a tire pressure gauge, a first aid kit, and more.

Or you can get a heavy-duty bag and build your own. Common Sense Home has a fabulous article on building a Winter Car Kit. And be sure to check out their article on building a custom first aid kit, which should also be part of your car kit.

Get-Home Bag (GHB)

Do you need a get-home bag? If you ever leave your home, chances are good you should add a get-home bag to your preparedness plans. This bag contains the emergency essentials you need in order to get from where you're stranded—work, running errands, a dentist appointment, grocery shopping—to your home. Building up your supplies at home is all well and good, but getting home safely is essential.

In preparedness circles, we often hear the term bug-out bag, or BOB. A BOB is a bag put together to get you to your bug-out location and usually designed to carry all you need for at least three days.

For many people, a get-home bag will be much smaller. Some people refer to these as twenty-four-hour bags since they contain only the items you need to get from the office to the house. I like to think of my get-home bag as a comfort bag. While it does contain supplies needed to safely return to my house and loved ones, it also has essential items to make life a little more comfortable.

Why You Need a Get-Home Bag

Don't think of a GHB as something that is only useful in the case of TEOTWAWKI (the end of the world as we know it). It can be helpful on many occasions.

I used to live outside of Portland, Oregon. On the rare occasions we'd get snow, there was a hill heading out of Portland on Highway 26 that would often have stranded cars. People couldn't get their vehicle up the hill, so they'd just stop—not even pulling off the highway sometimes. When 26 turned into a parking lot, people started walking. A GHB sure would've been helpful for them.

A get-home bag isn't something that you should stock and forget, saving it for the end of the world as we know it. Instead, it should be adjusted seasonally. Living in Wyoming, where the temperatures often dip, my winter bag focuses on warmth. Likewise, my summer bag has more sun and bug protection. Your GHB should also complement your Everyday Carry (EDC). Whew—the acronyms!

Also, because I live in Wyoming, my bag isn't set up as a twenty-four-hour bag. We have the smallest population in the US but are the tenth largest in size. Our towns tend to be long distances apart. Just going to the grocery store is a half-hour drive one way. If I needed to walk home from there, I'm looking at close to two days—and that's if all goes as planned.

You need a get-home bag, and you need it to be built to suit you. The suggestions below are ideas to get you started. Build your bag to fit your location, environment, and necessities.

The Bag

Start your GHB by choosing a suitable bag for you. A not-too-large backpack is the likely choice. You'll be stashing this in your car or truck, so it needs to fit. And you don't want it to be too big and bulky—it doesn't need to be since it's only packed for twenty-four hours or so. Something compact with sections and pockets is helpful but not essential. My first GHB was made out of an old school backpack since that is what I had at the time and it fit well in my small car.

Depending on your lifestyle, you may wish to have more than one GHB. Many people choose to stash one in their desk or locker at work. Do your children need one at school? That's something to consider.

You may also want to consider whether each person should have a GHB for the car or if you'll use a family bag.

We ski on the weekends. The ski lodge is about eighty miles from home. We pack one large bag with essentials and also have a small, empty foldable day pack and a foldable messenger bag (an old cloth bag I've had for years). The large bag can be redistributed among the three bags. And as my husband will tell you, I overpack the car for ski trips, too, so we'd have plenty of extra things to stuff in those bags. Which brings me to the next point...

Weight

BOBs are famous (or should I say infamous) for being packed to the gills with everything anyone can think of to survive. Many are packed so heavy there is no way the desired however many miles (usually too many) per day can be met. As a backcountry backpacker, I get the appeal of having everything you need in that pack. But it's just not possible. Same with your GHB—don't overpack. You want to get from point A to point B as quickly as possible. For most people, you won't have thirty or eighty miles to walk home. Pack what you need and be smart about it.

What to Put in Your Get-Home Bag

First Aid Kit

- Basic first aid kit: if purchasing a ready-made kit, you may need to add a few things such as burn dressings (large and small), a tourniquet, emergency bandages, a roll of gauze, vet wrap, etc. (keep the weight in mind, and pack only what you need)

- A pack of single-use super glue to close wounds
- Pain relievers: Tylenol and Aleve
- Personal prescriptions for the amount of time you are building your bag (plus maybe a little extra)

Lighting & Electronics

- Chem lights
- Headlamp or flashlight or ink pen with light
- Charger for your cell phone (home and car version)

Fire Starters

- Lighter, waterproof matches, waterproof fire starter, or something similar (more than one is always smart)

Food & Water

- Water purifying tablets, LifeStraw, or my favorite mini Sawyer (it's very versatile)
- Water bottle
- Freeze-dried food for the duration of your pack (or lots of snacks instead)
- Kind bars, Naked Nutrition Bars or Cookies, or something similar
- Cold drink mixes
- Hot drink mixes
- Hard candy
- Backpacker's stove if you are doing freeze-dried food (I like the kind that comes with pans and utensils)

Personal Hygiene

- Lip balm
- Tissues or cloth hanky
- Wet wipes

- Toothbrush, toothpaste, deodorant

Clothing

- A change of socks (or two)
- A change of underwear
- Walking shoes (essential if you wear dress shoes to work)
- Multifunctional gaiter or bandanna (great for bugs in summer or cold in winter, and it can also hold your hair back and keep sweat out of your eyes; you can also use it to filter water before purifying)
- Rain poncho (helpful even in winter as an extra layer, especially if you're not packing sleeping gear)
- Wool hat (seasonal)
- Gloves (seasonal)

Sleeping Gear

You may or may not need these based on your personal circumstances. For me, with my distances, they make sense.

- Emergency tent or lightweight backpacker's tent
- Backpacker's sleeping bag
- Emergency blankets
- Sleeping pad

Safety & Security

Safety and security items may also be part of your EDC. Add or subtract as needed.

- Multitool, pocketknife, or fixed blade
- Folding saw
- Emergency whistle with compass
- A paper map of your state and/or local area

- Self-defense tools

Miscellaneous Things

- Tarps (or make your bag lighter by cutting 3mm plastic to tarp size)
- Duct tape
- Small notepad
- Heavy-duty carabiner clip
- Paracord
- Small binoculars
- Zip ties
- Plastic bags
- Cash (small bills)

Bug-Out Bag (BOB)

A bug-out bag, commonly referred to as its acronym BOB, is often what people think of first when discussing survival. The idea behind the BOB is to have a supply of goods to be able to get you from your home to your bug-out location (BOL). It's almost always a large backpack and almost always fully loaded, and they're touted as a necessary item for all preppers. But are they?

Earlier in this book, I shared many reasons why you may want to start prepping. Most of these reasons are terribly mundane and localized. Very few of them are emergencies caused by a widescale event that would necessitate hiking many miles with everything you own on your back.

Hunker Down

The recent pandemic, an emergency situation by most standards, is a prime example of hunkering down. Those who went into the early days with some supplies on hand didn't need to fight over toilet paper. They didn't need to wait in lines while only a certain number of people were allowed to shop at a time. Having supplies on hand brought a degree of comfort.

Most emergencies, while not as widespread, would be similar. Job loss or other personal economic issues would be stay-at-home events, as opposed to bug-out events. As I think through possible emergencies where I may need to strap on my BOB, very few come to mind.

That doesn't mean I don't have a well-stocked backpack full of several days' worth of supplies—I do. But in my case, it's in the form of a get-home bag.

Of course, recent events on the world stage do show people carrying everything dear to them (including their pets) as they evacuate to safety. You should determine your need for a bug-out bag based on your specific situation. I'm always a fan of erring on the side of caution and being prepared for whatever may come.

Your Bug-Out Bag

There's much to consider when thinking of bugging out. Beyond what to put in your backpack, the first question is, where will you go? Do you have a bug-out location? Do you have a secondary location? A third option?

Most emergencies that may require you to bug out are going to be localized events: a hurricane, tornado, or fast-moving wildfire. Your bug-out location could be a friend's home out of the danger zone or a hotel across the state. In these types of emergencies, you won't be carrying your supplies on your back as you walk miles and miles, but rather driving your car or possibly riding in an evac vehicle of some sort.

My bug-out bag is not what you may expect from a longtime preparedness advocate. Considering I live very rurally, I've always thought it unlikely I'd bug out.

Unlikely, but possible.

That possibility happened in November of 2021 when we were evacuated in the middle of the night due to a fast-moving wildfire.

Your situation may be different. You may live in an urban area. You may have a bug-out location and have decided at the first sign of trouble you're out of there. If you have a car, taking it is the best choice, but also be prepared to walk (or bike) should you need to abandon your vehicle.

While I may not have a typical bug-out bag, my get-home bag is very similar. And as a backpacker, I'm familiar with the pitfalls of carrying several days' worth of gear. Here are a few tips to consider for your BOB.

Your Pack

Your pack should be well-fitted to your body. If you've ever looked at the large array of backpacks available, you'll see you have choices. One of the first choices is capacity. In most cases, the backpack size is listed in liters. It's tempting to choose the largest you can find and be done with it.

No matter how large your bag is, you can only carry so much weight. And trust me when I tell you that what doesn't feel terribly heavy when testing it in the living room will feel like a cannonball on the trail! When we first started backpacking, most websites suggested keeping the loaded pack weight at 20 percent of your body weight. So if you weigh 150 pounds, the pack should be under thirty pounds.

This is great advice if you're used to backpacking and are in excellent physical health. If you're new to carrying a pack around, 15 percent is a much more reasonable number. A pack weighing 22.5 pounds may not sound like much less than thirty pounds, but it is!

Tip: The first day, the thirty pounds doesn't feel terrible, but it goes downhill from there. Eat your heaviest food on day one.

Ideally, you should increase your fitness level to be able to accommodate the weight of the pack. You can only get your pack weight so low without losing necessary supplies. Keep in mind, weather plays a role in your gear too. If you switch out gear seasonally (and you should), your winter pack may be heavier than your summer pack.

What My Family Uses

For our wilderness treks, my husband uses an eighty-five-liter backpack. It holds enough gear for a week (or longer) and fits him perfectly. He's just shy of six feet tall and is two hundred plus pounds. I'm five-foot-two and weigh less than he does. While his pack was advertised as adjustable, it doesn't adjust down enough to fit me. But my sixty-five-liter pack is a near-perfect fit, sitting as it should and resting in all the right places.

Our son's pack is fifty-five-liter with an adjustable torso. It doesn't hold as much, but that makes sense considering he couldn't carry as much. Now he's a teenager and is taller than me. His pack still fits, but it's a little worn, so it's time for a new one. Finding a comfortable pack goes a long way.

How to Choose a Pack

While we choose backpacking-style packs, there are many backpacks on the market geared toward using as a bug-out bag as opposed to for recreation. If you're looking for a pack with more of a tactical feel, here's a great review of popular ones.

When choosing a pack, consider what it looks like. If you're leaving the city, you want to blend in with the crowd. As I watched videos of refugees fleeing Ukraine, I noticed most were wearing basic school backpacks while dragging rolling suitcases. There were several with large backpacking-style packs. Very few had tactical packs with MOLLE pouches.

If you want to blend into the crowd, consider your location. Keep color in mind too. A bright orange pack may be eye-catching, but is that what you want?

Where I live, backpacks are common accessories. Not eighty-five-liter packs for everyday use, but the tactical style is common. So are camouflaged packs. A camo tactical pack wouldn't get a second look in my area.

Packing Your Bug-Out Bag

If you're planning to live out of your backpack for several days, it should have the basics needed to be comfortable. As you are filling it, keep the weight in mind. Careful packing will also help with comfort. There are many helpful videos and articles on packing for long hikes.

Tip: When you think you have the "perfect" pack, test it out. Spend a night or two in the wilderness hiking around with the pack on during the day. How'd it feel? How was camp? What'd you forget? What could you do without?

Water

One liter of water weighs 2.2 pounds. A common backpacker's formula is one liter per two hours of hiking. This can vary based on conditions, but it gives a starting point. Doing the math of how many hours you need to walk to your bug-out location will likely show you can't carry enough water to get there.

You should carry water, yes. But you should also have a way to filter and purify more water. And you should know your route and places to find water.

For carrying water, you might want a hydration bladder, which stays inside your pack and you drink through a tube. If you haven't used one of these, you should definitely try it before you need it. I'm not a fan, but my son loves them.

Most backpacks have side pockets for carrying hard water bottles. Collapsible water bottles can also be a good choice. And many backpackers swear by Smart Water. They are widely available, filled with water when purchased, and have a nice thickness yet are lighter than hard bottles. You can even screw a Sawyer filter right on the bottle!

Because two is one and one is none, have multiple options for purifying water. It's a good idea to have purification tablets plus a bandanna or something to filter cloudy water (before purifying) or a straw-style filter.

Fire

For cooking and warmth, you should have several fire-starting options. A couple of basic lighters and strike-anywhere matches (kept in a waterproof container) are always a good idea. Add in a Ferro rod or other options as you wish.

You should also have a stove if you plan to cook. Backpacking stoves that run on fuel canisters are easy to use, but you should practice with them in advance. If you don't want to carry fuel, consider a wood-burning option.

Many backpacking stoves have companion cooking containers. You need this if you plan to cook food, heat water, etc.

Shelter

Many bug-out bag lists share emergency tents as an excellent option. And depending on your location, one of these or even just a tarp may be all the shelter you need. My problem with either an emergency tent or a tarp is needing a couple of trees to make them work. Trees are scarce in many parts of Wyoming!

We choose lightweight and inexpensive one or two-man tents. They are nothing fancy and won't hold up to prolonged use, but they are a good option. Look for a tent that weighs no more than 3 to 3.5 pounds, and choose a color that will blend into your surroundings.

Your clothing is also part of your shelter. You should have undergarments, a couple pairs of socks, comfortable sleeping clothes, and a change of clothes.

Your clothing should also be geared toward the season. In Wyoming, our winters are harsh. A base layer, middle layer, and outer layer are essential. I recently purchased the Fortress base layer. It's the best I've ever used for wicking away sweat. These are investment pieces, but you can get a discount when joining their newsletter. I plan on adding their outer layers (the Storm Bundle) next.

Changing out your clothing seasonally will help ensure you have what you need when you need it. It's also a great way to check sizes and make sure everything is in excellent condition.

What about a sleeping bag or blanket? Again, this could change from season to season. Determine your needs and plan accordingly. Throwing in an emergency blanket or two is a good idea. Remember, the silver crinkly type works in a way that traps your own body heat. I've found using one is a different experience than a regular blanket. And they're noisy.

Food

You can expect to burn 700 to 1,200 calories on a ten-mile walk. If you're going uphill or are under stress, you may burn more. Food adds weight to your pack but is necessary. For backpacking, we figure each day's worth of food will add somewhere around two pounds. How many days will it take you to walk to your bug-out location? Use this to determine how much food you will need to carry.

Lightweight, nutrient-dense food is best. Many people choose freeze-dried backpacking meals. While lightweight, they do require water and, preferably, fire to make them edible. Many are also high in salt, making you need more water. You might consider dehydrating your own backpacking meals.

Backpacking Chef has many great tips, and I learned a lot from the book *The Hungry Spork: A Long-Distance Hiker's Guide to Meal Planning*, which has suggestions on combining freeze-dried, dehydrated, and packaged foods. You might even consider some canned goods, knowing you will eat those first.

And olive oil.

We always carry olive oil. It has 250 calories in an ounce and a multitude of uses, not all of them cooking. On one trip, a bug flew in my ear. We used olive oil to get it to stop buzzing around. What an experience that was.

We really like the protein bars from Naked Nutrition. Each bar contains 15 grams of protein (from grass-fed whey). The calories keep it in the snack range (180 for chocolate, 190 for peanut butter). Another lightweight option is ration bars. These contain 2,400 to 3,600 calories per bar, but…oh my. The taste isn't there, and you need a huge glass of water to wash it down.

Survival Supplies

Yes, we've already been talking about these. Water, fire, shelter, food…definitely all for survival. This section is a catchall of other things you should consider.

- Knife and/or multitool
- Rope (a length of paracord is great)
- First aid kit or trauma kit (know how to use everything in your kit)
- Flashlight or headlamp (with a red light plus extra batteries)
- Personal hygiene items
- Necessary medications (have enough for your estimated time to your bug-out location plus extra)
- Paper map(s) of the area you are traveling
- Personal tool for self-defense

Documents

While most of your personal identification documents will be included in your Everyday Carry (such as your driver's license), it's a good idea to keep copies of them and things like insurance information (car, house, etc.). If you own your bug-out location, it's a good idea to have proof of ownership (copy of your land title, mortgage docs) or rental agreement. Same for the house you are leaving. Also, consider having a copy of your will and other legal documents. Whatever can make your life easier in the long run.

Finding Storage Space

As you build your food storage and non-food supplies, consider where you're going to put everything. Most of us don't want flats of canned goods in the living room.

Start with what you have. Organize your pantry and cabinets. Pull everything out, then wipe down the shelves and put things away. Keeping like items together, just like in a grocery store, is very helpful. Check the Resources section to learn my process for annually organizing my pantry.

Once everything is neat and organized, you'll probably find you have a lot more room than you expected. You can also do the same things with your pots and pans. There's no rule that you can't tuck a few containers of rice in with your pans!

When thinking about where to store your shelf-stable foods, consider the climate. Your food should be kept in an area that is somewhat climate-controlled and has low light. Canned goods (both commercial and home-canned) should not be exposed to extreme temperatures. Home-canned seals can break, and commercial cans can bulge.

An attic likely gets too hot in the summer months for food storage (consider this space for other things like toilet paper and bandages). Your garage may also get too hot and/or too cold. Or you may wish to consider a nifty air-conditioned, insulated pantry in your garage like the Prudent Homemaker has. If you have a basement, this might be an ideal space to add a few shelves or freestanding cabinets for storage.

For most of us, even after organizing and sorting, we need to find additional storage space to meet our goals. How about the bedroom closet? Is it cool and dark? Can you eek out a little space by adding narrow shelves? In our previous house, I kept my ferments on shelves in the master closet. It was cold like a root cellar and was the perfect space. Under the bed may also work for you, especially if you use the little riser things to lift the bed slightly so flat totes can fit underneath.

Adding a label on the visible edge of the tote will make your life easier. This label could be general (such as *canned goods*) or might correspond with a spreadsheet or notebook for additional details. Find a system that works best for your personality, but do try and mark your containers in some way so you don't have to pull everything out to find what you're looking for.

Our closet and under-bed storage are also subject to the first in, first out (FIFO) rotation. When my kitchen shelf is running low on coconut milk, I shop the tote first, replenishing from there, then buying new products to refill the tote.

When we were designing our current home, we added a few built-in storage locations. At our previous house, storage space was extremely limited, and we used many different methods—not only under the beds but also a multitude of other places. Remember, you can store food anywhere, not just in the kitchen.

We've used the following places for storage:

- We added curtains to freestanding shelves in our living room that we used to hold five-gallon buckets (metal shelves can be reconfigured slightly for size).
- Bookshelves were put behind the couch and used for canned goods (scoot the couch up tight against them).
- We added a row of cans behind books on bookshelves.
- I was given a wooden armoire that we reworked to hold cans and boxes.

- Freestanding shelves were added in the laundry room for water storage.
- Closets were reconfigured to add shelving for food storage.
- We did a lot of dehydrating (dehydrated goods shrink down and take up less space).
- Anything that could be stored in the garage (not temperature controlled) was put in the rafters.

Other storage spaces you might consider:

- Fill totes and stack them on top of each other, then cover them with a pretty cloth to make a side table or nightstand.
- If you store mason jars, fill them with grains, pasta, water...just about anything instead of storing them empty.
- Look for any nook and cranny to add shelves or storage units. The space between the fridge and the wall may be large enough for a roll-out shelving unit (ready-made or custom-built).
- Storage ottomans are great! I have them in my living room and office.
- Do you have stairs? Can you use the space underneath?
- Is there space above your kitchen cabinets? Can you put items in baskets or pretty boxes there?
- If you're looking to get creative, consider cutting into the back of your sofa and adding shelves to store lightweight items. Or you could open up a section of a wall, add shelves, and put a hinged mirror/door across the front.
- An old freezer may work as a root cellar or to store five-gallon buckets.
- Do you have a crawl space? Can it be utilized for storing buckets or totes?
- Do you have a like-minded friend or family member who (preferably) lives nearby? Can you team up and share storage space?

How to Bring all the Preparedness Tips Together

Getting started with preparedness can seem overwhelming. Even if you've come up with a general plan of what to do and how to do it, the trees can often get in the way of the forest. With the current situation of the world, the feeling of urgency can make you want to complete everything now. To help keep your financial house in order, and not have waste, it's smart to know *how* to move forward. These preparedness tips will help you figure out what's next.

I truly believe if you plan your work and work your plan, the long-term results will be worth it. Make no mistake, there are a lot of components to well-rounded preparedness. Please do not think you must do everything at once. That would be crazy overwhelming! Pick one or two things to focus on before moving on.

At the very least, please start on your water storage, quickly build to thirty days of basic easy-to-cook food, and have cash on hand for things like groceries, gas, and more.

Every planned effort you make today, no matter how seemingly small, can be a benefit in the long run. Do what you can do and give the rest to God.

"Who of you by worrying can add a single hour to your life?"
~ Luke 12:25

Resources

Check out the Resources page that goes along with this book for more tips, information, and helpful tools:

HomespunOasis.com/BeginnersResources.

Find more preparedness information on my website: HomespunOasis.com

Also by Millie Copper

Get 20% off Millie Copper's nonfiction eBooks at HomespunOasis.com/Books with coupon code SAVE20.

No-Cook Meals for Your Food Storage: An Affordable Way to Add Nutrition and Variety to Your Pantry

Want to make delicious, healthy no-cook meals that your whole family will love?

No-Cook Meals for Your Food Storage will show you how! Not only will you learn how to make quick meals without any cooking odors, but you'll also save time, energy, and fuel costs while still feeding your family wholesome, nutritious meals.

Sprouts for Your Food Storage: Add Nutrition and Variety to Your Diet

Want to make delicious, healthy sprouts that your whole family will love?

Sprouts For Your Food Storage will show you how! Sprouts are an easy, cheap, and tasty vegetable anyone can grow. They require little space and can be done without any special equipment. Because the original product grows during the sprouting process, this is a great way to stretch a small amount into a larger amount.

Sourdough for Your Food Storage: Add Nutrition and Variety to Your Baked Goods

Want to make tasty treats your whole family will love? Are you looking for a great way to expand your food storage grains?

Sourdough For Your Food Storage will show you how! Not only will you learn how to make delicious, crusty breads, but also biscuits, main dishes, and even desserts! Sourdough is a healthier alternative to yeast, and it tastes great to boot.

Real Food Hits the Road: Budget-Friendly Tips, Ideas, and Recipes for Enjoying Real Food Away from Home

Are you planning to hit the road for a family vacation? Do you want to take a road trip, but the idea of eating out three meals a day doesn't work for your budget or your health?

Real Food Hits the Road will be your guide to saving the budget, keeping your digestion working well, and eating real food away from home while letting you enjoy the trip and not "cook" all of the time.

Stock the Real Food Pantry: Save Money and Time While Gaining Peace of Mind

Do you want to stock your pantry with nutritious food your family will actually eat? In these trying times, are you focusing on your food storage?

If so, *Stock the Real Food Pantry* has you covered. Learn how a wonderfully stocked real food pantry will save you money and time— while giving you peace of mind.

Design a Dish: Save Your Food Dollars!

Would you like to learn great methods to reduce food waste? What if you could enjoy one meal for "free" each week?

Design a Dish will teach you how to make wonderful, simple dishes you can prepare day in and day out. You'll be amazed at how easy it is to nourish your family with these tasty dishes!

Stretchy Beans: Nutritious, Economical Meals the Easy Ways

Do you struggle with feeding your family delicious, healthy meals? Are you tired of trying to figure out what's for dinner each night? Do you cringe when you see how much money your family spends on groceries each month?

If so, *Stretchy Beans* is the solution you've been looking for! Learn how to easily prepare dinners that the whole family will love—while staying on budget, spending less time in the kitchen, and not losing your sanity.

About the Author

Millie Copper, writer of Cozy Apocalyptic Fiction and preparedness mentor, was born in Nebraska but never lived there. Her parents fully embraced wanderlust and moved regularly, giving her an advantage of being from nowhere and everywhere.

Millie Copper lives in the wilds of Wyoming with her husband and young son, tending chickens and attempting a food forest on their small homestead. After living off the grid for several years, they've recently gone back on the grid. Four adult daughters, three sons-in-law, and five grandchildren round out the family.

Since 2009, Millie has authored articles on traditional foods, alternative health, homesteading, and preparedness-many times all within the same piece. Millie has penned seven nonfiction, traditional food focused books, sharing how, with a little creativity, anyone can transition to a real foods diet without overwhelming their food budget.

The twelve-installment *Havoc in Wyoming* and six-installment *Montana Mayhem* Christian Post-Apocalyptic fiction series use her homesteading, off-the-grid, and preparedness lifestyle as a guide. The adventures continue in the *Dakota Destruction* series.

Find Millie at MillieCopper.com and HomespunOasis.com
Facebook: www.facebook.com/MillieCopperAuthor/
Amazon: www.amazon.com/author/MillieCopper
BookBub: https://www.bookbub.com/authors/Millie-Copper

www.ingramcontent.com/pod-product-compliance
Lightning Source LLC
Chambersburg PA
CBHW022105020426
42335CB00012B/835